Families Change

Praise for *Kids Need to Be Safe* from the Kids Are Important Series

"*Kids Need to Be Safe* is incredibly well done!
It is much different from all of the other books for children in foster care that I have read."
—Karen Jorgenson, Executive Director, National Foster Parent Association

"Julie Nelson demonstrates remarkable sensitivity to the needs and feelings of young children in foster care.
I'm confident that countless young children will draw strength and comfort from the clear
and simple words Ms. Nelson has written for them. And foster parents and other caregivers
will find a wealth of wisdom in the information provided for them, particularly in the
'healing words' to use when children are feeling confused and afraid."
**—Martha Farrell Erickson, Ph.D., Senior Fellow & Co-Chair,
President's Initiative on Children, Youth & Families, University of Minnesota**

"This is a wonderful book for foster parents to read to children so they understand why they are in foster care."
—Christa Misiewicz, Social Worker

"*Kids Need to Be Safe* is such a wonderful resource for us as well as our children! We are forwarding the order form
you enclosed to our foster parent association in hopes that they will get a copy for all of our foster families!"
—Sonya Sheppard, Senior Foster Care Caseworker

"Julie Nelson is a gifted teacher with a keen understanding of children's needs for ongoing,
unconditional emotional support. Her book underscores how important it is for adults to invite
children to express their feelings—all of them, including anger and fear—and to explain
and interpret adult behavior in terms that children can comprehend."
—Christopher Watson, Center for Early Education & Development, University of Minnesota

Families Change

A Book for Children Experiencing Termination of Parental Rights

BY JULIE NELSON

ILLUSTRATED BY MARY GALLAGHER

★ Kids Are Important Series
Help for Troubled Times

free spirit
PUBLiSHiNG®

Helping kids
help themselves™
since 1983

Library of Congress Cataloging-in-Publication Data
Nelson, Julie.
   Families change : a book for children experiencing termination of parental rights / by Julie Nelson ; illustrations by Mary Gallagher.
      p. cm. — (Kids are important)
      ISBN-13: 978-1-57542-209-1
      ISBN-10: 1-57542-209-3
1. Foster children—United States—Juvenile literature. 2. Adopted children—United States—Juvenile literature. 3. Problem families—United States—Juvenile literature. I. Gallagher, Mary, 1954 Dec. 16– II. Title. III. Series.
   HV881.N43 2006
   362.73'30973—dc22

                                                                                    2006011755

At the time of this book's publication, all facts and figures cited are the most current available. All telephone numbers, addresses, and Web site URLs are accurate and active; all publications, organizations, Web sites, and other resources exist as described in this book; and all have been verified as of April 2006. The author and Free Spirit Publishing make no warranty or guarantee concerning the information and materials given out by organizations or content found at Web sites, and we are not responsible for any changes that occur after this book's publication. If you find an error or believe that a resource listed here is not as described, please contact Free Spirit Publishing. Parents, teachers, and other adults: We strongly urge you to monitor children's use of the Internet.

Edited by Eric Braun
Cover and interior design by Marieka Heinlen

10 9 8 7 6 5 4 3 2 1
Printed in Hong Kong

Free Spirit Publishing Inc.
217 Fifth Avenue North, Suite 200
Minneapolis, MN 55401-1299
(612) 338-2068
help4kids@freespirit.com
www.freespirit.com

Dedication

This book is dedicated to our parents,
Edward and Johanna Gallagher and Ginger and Luvy Nelson.

Acknowledgments

Thank you to those who supported this project: Lalu and Daniel Abebe; Jodi Bantley;
Esmerald and Gina Theile; Eufemia Alvarado; Olive Fay; Anika, Christopher, Nevaeh, and
little Christopher Sangster-Lamb; Maddie and Mark Granlund; Melinda and Jasmine Wurl;
Heather and Brent Schley; Kristin Muyskens; Beth Nickels; Laura Nystrom; and Judith Julig.
Thank you also to Wendy Negaard; Kris Johnson; Linda Schlichte, M.S.W., L.I.C.S.W.;
and Jan Goetz, M.S.W., for reading drafts of the manuscript and providing feedback.

Author's Note

Each child's life experience is unique. Adult readers
of this book are encouraged to adapt the language
to match the needs and experience of the individual
child. If a child has experienced chronic abuse from
parents, consult a therapist who understands the
child's history to discuss what messages about
family history will best support the child's healing.

All families change.

A family changes when someone new
joins the family.

Sometimes a baby is born
or a grown-up gets married.

Sometimes a child gets a new foster parent
or new adopted mom or dad.

A family changes when someone leaves the family.

Someone in the family might move
or be gone for a long time.

Moms or dads or brothers or sisters
might be away at college,
in the army, in the hospital, in jail,
or in treatment.

Families change because people in them change.

Kids get bigger.

They change from babies to kids to teenagers to adults.

Adults change too.

All families change.

Some changes are happy.

Some changes are sad.

Some changes are happy and sad at the same time.

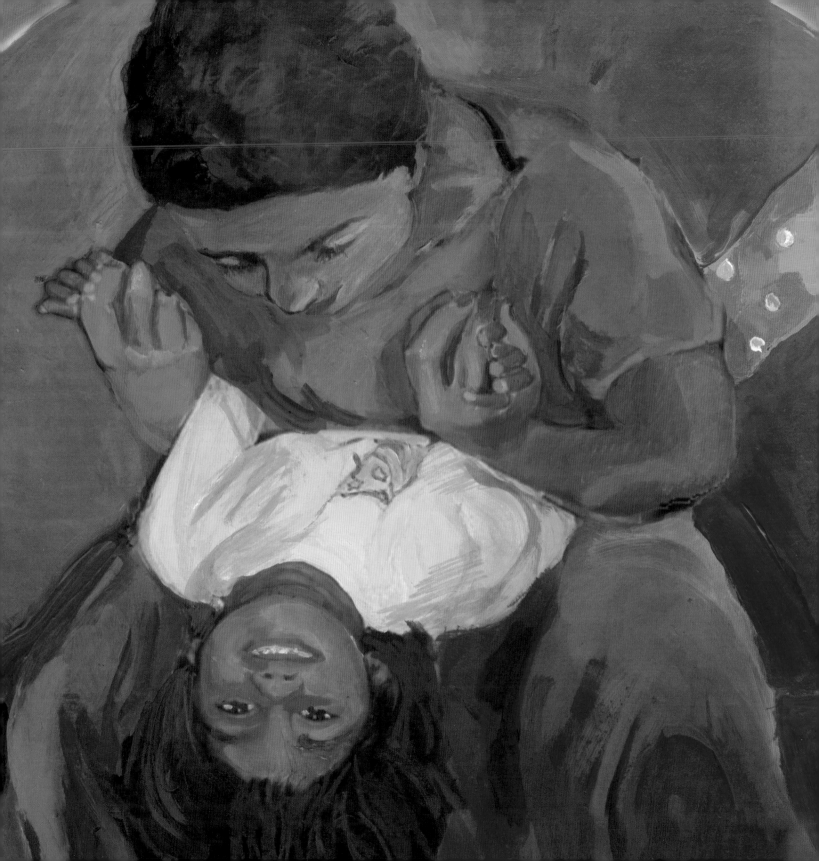

Sometimes families change in big ways,
and kids might have more than one mom or dad.

Kids might have a birth mom
who took care of them when they were little
and a foster mom who helped take care of them
when they were bigger.

They might have an adopted mom
who is a new everyday mom.

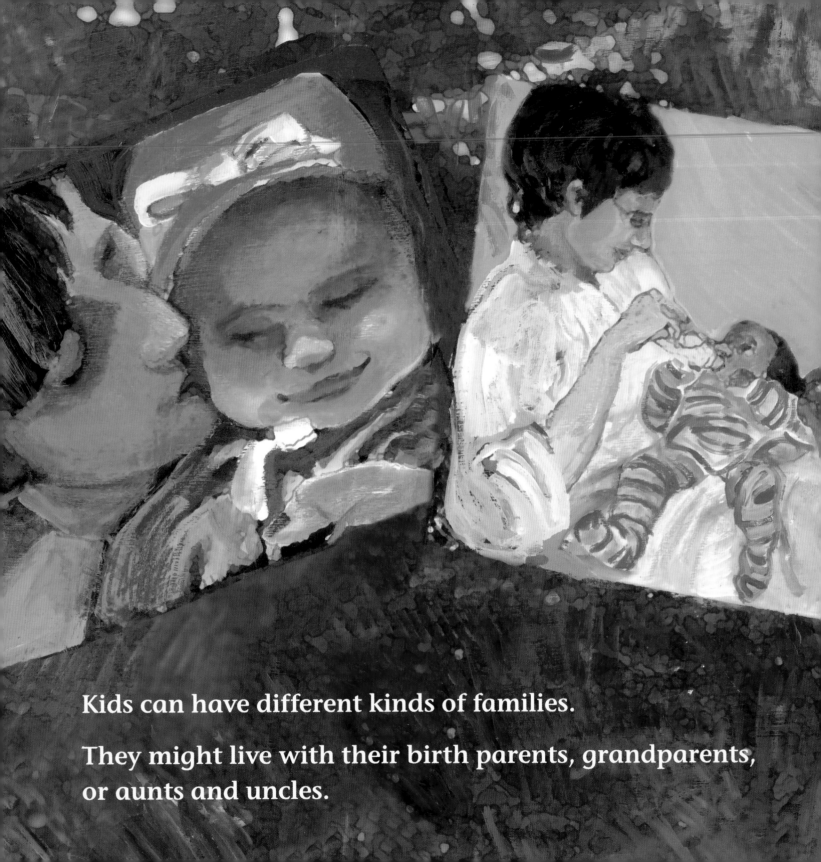

Kids can have different kinds of families.

They might live with their birth parents, grandparents, or aunts and uncles.

They might have foster families or adopted families.

All these families are real families.

All these families are important families.

Sometimes families have big problems to solve.

Kids and parents might need help
with their problems.

These big problems are never the kids' fault!

When problems hurt kids, families need to change
so kids will be safe.

A child's family might change
from a birth family
to a grandparent family
or a foster family
or an adoptive family.

Birth parents might feel mad or sad or worried when their family changes.

But birth parents want their children to be happy.

Birth parents want their children to have a safe home.

When families change,
kids can remember the happy times
and the sad and mad and scary times too.

Kids can remember
and love their birth families.

Kids can love their new families too.

Providing Support and Encouragement to Young Children Experiencing Termination of Parental Rights

A message to parents, foster parents, social workers, teachers, and caregivers

Taking care of children who have been removed from their parents' care is a challenging, exhausting, but rewarding task. Young children depend on their relationships with caregivers to validate them. When these relationships include abuse or neglect, or when the relationships are disrupted, children's sense of self-worth, trust, and safety suffer. In addition, termination of parental rights is a trauma that causes grief, stress, and a profound sense of loss, and many children have experienced the additional trauma of multiple placements. Children who have been through this pain may be hard to connect with and are likely to test your commitment to them. But with patience and perseverance you can establish a nurturing, trusting relationship. Use the following guidelines to show children they are important and safe. Remember, professional help is available for you and the children in your care.

ANSWER QUESTIONS

A child experiencing termination of parental rights will have questions and worries about the past, present, and future. *What happened? Is it my fault? Am I safe? Are the important people in my life safe? Will I see my parents again? Who will take care of me? Can I trust you?* Children may ask you some questions directly, while you will see others in their play or in their behavior. As a caring adult, you may wish to protect children from the difficult events that led to the termination of parental rights, but not explaining what has happened may cause children to blame themselves or their foster parents for the change and loss. Instead, invite children to ask questions. Answer them simply and honestly, with respect for their birth family. When you answer children's questions, you help them understand and cope with changes in their lives.

HELP MANAGE STRESS

The stress of family change can be overwhelming. Besides losing their parents, children may lose other family members, their home, toys, clothing, pets, and daily routines. Some children act out from the stress of these losses, screaming, throwing toys, or hitting. Some children shut down by hiding their feelings and rarely talking. The stress children experience is physical, and they may appear hyperactive or have stomachaches, headaches, or difficulty sleeping. Physical exercise and sensory activities such as playing with water or clay can help relieve stress. Encourage outdoor play and other forms of physical activity. You also can reduce stress and help children feel safe and calm by providing predictable, nurturing daily routines. For example, you might eat breakfast together each morning, talk about your day each evening at dinner, and read a story together each night before bed.

UNDERSTAND TRAUMA

Children who experience termination of parental rights often have had other traumatic life experiences. They may have been subjected to family violence, community violence, physical abuse, or sexual abuse. Consider professional therapy to help children's healing. Understand their trauma and be patient when they exhibit behavior that stems from it. Such behavior—and supportive ways to react to it—includes:

- *Hypervigilance.* Children may watch their world closely for signs of danger or loss. Certain sounds or touches, or people coming or leaving, may cause them to worry. Reassure children by patiently explaining what is happening and reminding them they are safe.

- *Flashbacks.* Experiences in the present may trigger emotions from children's past. If children react to a situation much more intensely than seems appropriate, those emotions may be about the past, not the present. Empathize with children's overwhelming emotions while teaching them to regulate the intensity of their reactions so they're more in line with what currently is happening. It may help to say things like, "When there is a little problem, you can be a little mad," or "I can be your partner when you are having really big feelings."

- *Identifying with the aggressor.* Children who have witnessed or been the victim of violence may struggle with feelings of helplessness. They may want to be as strong as the person who caused the hurt, and they may imitate this person to keep from feeling vulnerable. Talk to children about ways they can be strong and safe without being aggressive.

HONOR THE CHILD'S PAST

Children's birth families and birth culture will always be important to them. Help children feel positive about who they are by embracing their heritage and their past. Talk with them about their culture and history. You also can create a memory book, celebrating where the child was born and remembering important people and events in the child's life. Help the child share memories for the book by asking simple questions about toys, foods, places, people, or pets that have been a part of his or her life before coming to you.

BUILD A TRUSTING RELATIONSHIP

Children need positive, stable relationships with the adults who care for them in order to develop a sense of security and self-worth. Since children who have been abused or neglected or who have lost relationships with important people in their lives may have difficulty trusting adults, forming a trusting relationship will take time. Play with the child, laugh with the child, and respond to the child's requests for caregiving with warmth and consistency.

With the support of caring adults, children who are hurting can move from the pain of the past to the promise of the future. Thank you for your support of children.

Hurt, Hope, and Healing
Supporting children who have experienced termination of parental rights

About 50,000 children are adopted from the foster care system in the United States each year, and another 100,000 children are waiting for adoptive homes. Supporting young children in our communities who have been impacted by stress and trauma is an investment in the future. High-quality support of at-risk children can increase school success, reduce criminal justice involvement, and encourage healthy relationships. The economic benefits of early intervention and help far exceed the costs. The children, their foster and adoptive parents, and their teachers and caregivers all need support and information. Resources for understanding and meeting the needs of young children experiencing the termination of parental rights include:

Child Trauma Academy

The Child Trauma Academy is a nonprofit organization whose mission is to help improve the lives of traumatized and maltreated children in three primary ways: education, service delivery, and program consultation. The article "Helping Traumatized Children," as well as other free resources, is available at the academy's Web site, www.childtrauma.org. Free online courses, including "Surviving Childhood: An Introduction to the Impact of Trauma," "The Cost of Caring: Secondary Traumatic Stress and the Impact of Working with High-Risk Children and Families," and "Bonding and Attachment in Maltreated Children," are available at www.childtraumaacademy.com.

Child Welfare League of America (CWLA)

CWLA works to promote the well-being of children, youth, and their families, and to protect children from harm through training, consultation, conferences, publications, and other membership services. It also advocates for public policies at every level that contribute to the well-being of children, youths, families, and neighborhoods. To learn more about CWLA, and to access free online periodicals (such as *Children's Monitor*, which provides the latest information on federal legislation, regulations, and policy affecting children, youth, and families), go to www.cwla.org.

Court Appointed Special Advocates (CASA)

CASA volunteers advocate for abused and neglected children in court to ensure they do not suffer further abuse due to the overburdened court system or at home. Today, more than 900 CASA program offices are in operation. Go to their Web site, www.nationalcasa.org, for information, newsletters, volunteer opportunities, and more.

Gray, Deborah D. *Attaching in Adoption: Practical Tools for Today's Parents.* Indianapolis, IN: Perspectives Press, 2002.

This book explains attachment and offers ways to overcome challenges in achieving attachment. It is particularly helpful for families involved in interracial and cross-cultural adoptions, families adopting older children, abused or neglected children, and children from foster programs.

The Infant-Parent Institute

The Infant-Parent Institute is dedicated to understanding the relationship between early social experiences and development. It offers clinical services and professional training and conducts research related to the optimal development of infants and their families. The institute has developed 14 training videos, including "Breaking Peaces: Babies Have Their Say About Domestic Violence," "Multiple Transitions: A Young Child's Point of View on Foster Care and Adoption," and "Is Anyone In There? Adopting a Wounded Child." More information about the Infant-Parent Institute, including how to order videos, can be found at www.infant-parent.com.

Keck, Gregory C., and Regina M. Kupecky. *Adopting the Hurt Child: Hope for Families with Special-Needs Kids: A Guide for Parents and Professionals.* **Colorado Springs: NavPress Publishing Group, 1998.**

A source of valuable information, hope, and inspiration for adoptive and foster parents, teachers, therapists, social workers, and all others whose lives interact with hurt children.

The National Foster Parent Association (NFPA)

NFPA is a national organization that strives to support foster parents, and is a consistently strong voice on behalf of all children. Information and many resources, including training and education, are available at www.nfpainc.org.

Prevent Child Abuse America (PCA America)

PCA America works to build awareness, provide education, and inspire hope in everyone involved in the effort to prevent the abuse and neglect of children. It raises awareness about child abuse through research, initiatives, national publications, and national and local events. Its Web site is www.preventchildabuse.org.

About Lifetrack Resources and Families Together

For more than 50 years, Lifetrack Resources has provided services that make a life-changing difference for children and adults with serious challenges to independence and self-sufficiency. Support is provided in the areas of:

- early childhood education and family support
- employment
- rehabilitation therapies

Lifetrack Resources' mission is to build better lives by working together to develop people's strengths. For more information please contact:

Lifetrack Resources
709 University Avenue West
St. Paul, Minnesota 55104-4804
651-227-8471
www.lifetrackresources.org
familiestogether@lifetrackresources.org

Families Together is a therapeutic preschool and home visiting program that applies current research on effective early intervention for highly stressed, abused, and neglected children.

About the Author and Illustrator

Julie Nelson holds a B.A. in psychology, is a licensed early childhood teacher, and has graduate certification in Child Abuse Prevention Studies. She has taught in at-risk early childhood settings for most of her 30-year professional career and is currently the senior teacher at Lifetrack Resources' Families Together program. She also provides training in working with highly stressed, hurting, and challenging children, including training presentations at National Association for the Education of Young Children (NAEYC), the Child Welfare League of America conference, Minnesota Association for the Education of Young Children (MnAEYC), Minnesota Children's Mental Health Conference, and Head Start, and in college settings. Julie is passionate about and committed to supporting society's most highly stressed children: those who are in foster care, who are homeless, who have been abused, and/or whose parents are incarcerated or struggle with substance abuse.

Mary Gallagher holds an M.F.A. in studio arts and an M.A. in occupational therapy. She has been a pediatric occupational therapist for seven years, working in St. Paul charter schools and at Families Together. She exhibited her paintings in the Twin Cities and in New York City for ten years after completing her degree at the City University of New York in 1989. In recent years, she has focused primarily on creating art installations in public spaces and illustrating books in order to reach a wider, more diverse audience.

Also available in the Kids Are Important Series

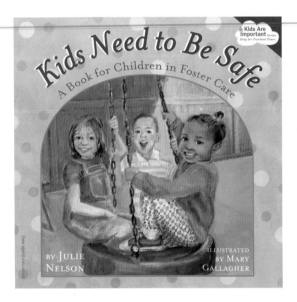

KIDS NEED TO BE SAFE
by Julie Nelson, illustrated by Mary Gallagher

"Kids are important. They need safe places to live, and safe places to play." For some kids, this means living with foster parents. In simple words and full-color illustrations, this book explains why some kids move to foster homes, what foster parents do, and ways kids might feel during foster care. Children often believe that they are in foster care because they are "bad." This book makes it clear that the troubles in their lives are not their fault; the message throughout is one of hope and support. Includes resources and information for parents, foster parents, social workers, counselors, and teachers. For ages 4–10.
32 pp.; color illustrations; softcover; 9" x 9"

Fast, Friendly, and Easy to Use

www.freespirit.com

- Browse the catalog
- Info & extras
- Many ways to search
- Quick check-out
- Stop in and see!

For a fast and easy way to receive our practical tips, helpful information, and special offers, send your email address to upbeatnews@freespirit.com. View a sample letter and our privacy policy at www.freespirit.com.

1.800.735.7323 • fax 612.337.5050 • help4kids@freespirit.com